BRITAIN IN OLD PHOTOGRAPHS

WORDSWORTH'S LAKELAND

JOHN MARSH & JOHN GARBUTT

VERITAS.

WORDSWORTH.

BORN AT COCKERMOUTH.1770.

SUTTON PUBLISHING LIMITED

Sutton Publishing Limited
Phoenix Mill · Thrupp · Stroud
Gloucestershire · GL5 2BU

First published 1997

Photograph, page 1: The arms of William
Wordsworth, with the three church bells and
the crest of an antelope's head, appeared on
early postcards. The motto 'Veritas' (truth)
was also included.

British Library Cataloguing in Publication Data
A catalogue record for this book is available from the
British Library.

ISBN 0-7509-1576-5

Typeset in 10/12 Perpetua.
Typesetting and origination by
Sutton Publishing Limited.
Printed in Great Britain by
Ebenezer Baylis, Worcester.

This book is dedicated to the many Friends and helpers at
'The Armitt', Ambleside.

Where it all began. Sockbridge House, Tirril, the home of Richard and Mary, William's grandparents,
'the first of the name in Westmorland'.

CONTENTS

This painting of the poet by Haydon was reproduced as a very early colour postcard by the Pictorial Stationery Co. of London in their Peacock Postcard series. Other prints of the poet at various ages appear on most chapter opening pages.

INTRODUCTION

The death of William Wordsworth in 1850 coincided with the birth of photography. There is a copy of a daguerreotype of Wordsworth from the 1840s which was rephotographed by local early Grasmere photographer R. Carlyle. This reproduction is now in the Wordsworth Museum at Dove Cottage, Grasmere. The early postcard photographers, realising the commercial value of Wordsworth, reproduced many nineteenth-century drawings and paintings of the poet and his circle of friends on cards for sale to the tourist. We include a number of these at various places in our book.

The Lakeland that Wordsworth knew and about which he wrote so much had not experienced the publicity that the camera was soon to provide, but was, in the middle of the nineteenth century, undergoing a transition from wilderness to 'Elysium' with the 'romantic movement' and improved transport stimulating tourism, an industry that is now paramount. In this book the authors use photographs from the late decades of the nineteenth century and the early decades of the twentieth century to illustrate Wordsworth's Lakeland people, places and scenery, in a medium far removed from the etchings and poetic and artistic licence that the poet had experienced – although the faking of photographs to render a scene sublime also became an art form.

In his last years the poet became a savage reactionary as there were attempts to harm his Utopia, and yet in his youth he had written one of the earliest of guides to the Lake District, which ran into many money-making reprints and undoubtedly produced the interest that caused a lot of the problems he saw in popular tourism. He penned the lines now so often quoted by conservationists, 'Is there no nook of English ground secure?', and used the words to attack the proposed Kendal to Windermere Railway in 1844; at the same time, however, he instructed his solicitor to buy him shares in the new railway companies. In his early years Wordsworth extolled a Republic of Shepherds in the Lake District but then, as holder of a '£400 a year sinecure', became a local tax collector through his work at the Ambleside Stamp Office. In early adult years he supported the French Revolution, hated aristocrats, especially the Lowther family from near Penrith, and was in every way a Whig revolutionary. In his middle and old ages he turned all these views on their head and became a reactionary Tory, sycophantic to the

Lowthers and hater of the Brougham family, who were instrumental in the Whig Reform Acts that so changed the Britain of the 1830s. He spent his latter years wondering out loud what the world was coming to, while nursing the secret of his bastard daughter by a Catholic royalist lady – whom he had met on a youthful visit to revolutionary France to support the anti-royalist cause.

His work as a poet, along with his friends Coleridge and Southey (forming the Lakeland School), also changed the Lakes in that the poets became, and have remained, a centre of the tourism they so much deplored. Influential people also bought land to build houses in and around Grasmere to experience the joys of the district that Wordsworth wrote and spoke about so much. He encouraged some people he knew to do this, although he despised one development (at Allan Bank) completely. He later became friendly with the family at Allan Bank and even rented the place for a time.

Wordsworth was a man of as many contrasts as the Lakeland of his time. Hunter Davies's biography of William Wordsworth (first published by Weidenfeld & Nicolson in 1980 and now reissued in paperback by Sutton Publishing) takes the reader through the contortions of the poet's life in an easily readable style and we recommend the book to anyone wishing to discover more about Wordsworth, the man, his family, friends and their times.

Following the death of Wordsworth in 1850 many things were to happen in the Grasmere and Ambleside area that further enhanced the district as a centre of literary and artistic matters. John Ruskin, R.G. Collingwood, Beatrix Potter, H.D. Rawnsley, Charlotte Mason, Mary Armitt, Harriet Martineau, William Green and, much later, Arthur Ransome all played their part in attracting even more interest to the area. In 1828 William Wordsworth was a member of the Ambleside Book Society, which in 1912 amalgamated with the Ambleside Ruskin Library (founded in 1882) to form the Armitt Library, a wish expressed in the will of Mary Louisa Armitt. The Armitt Library has, only this year, found a permanent home for its magnificent collection, and can now display to the public its unique collection of books and artifacts associated with the Ambleside area. This collection includes the amazing photographic archive of Herbert Bell, the Ambleside chemist, which we have been allowed to draw on for many of the pictures in our book.

John Marsh and John Garbutt
September 1997

HOME & SCHOOL
– EARLY DAYS

William Wordsworth painted by W. Shuter in 1798.

William Wordsworth was born in this house in Main Street, Cockermouth, on 7 April 1770. His father, John, was the agent of Sir James Lowther ('Wicked Jimmy') of Lowther Castle. This house and William's mother's family home in Penrith (see p. 10) were to be the focus of his childhood years.

My heart leaps up when I behold
A rainbow in the sky:
So was it when my life began;
So it is now I am a man;
So be it when I shall grow old,
Or let me die!
The Child is father of the Man;
And I could wish my days to be
Bound each to each by natural piety.

Wordsworth's Birthplace, Cockermouth

Cockermouth lies at the confluence of the rivers Cocker and Derwent. In 'The Prelude' we read:

> When, having left his Mountains, to the Towers
> Of Cockermouth that beauteous River came,
> Behind my Father's House he passed, close by,
> Along the margin of our terraced walk,
> He was a playmate whom we dearly lov'd.

William Cookson was a linen draper in Penrith. His daughter, Ann, born in 1747, became the wife of John Wordsworth and the poet's mother. Their business premises and house, much altered since the eighteenth century, can be seen at the top of the market-place in this Edwardian photograph. Here William's mother died on 8 March 1778 aged thirty, when he was eight years old. Dorothy and William attended the Penrith dame school run by Ann Birkett.

Hawkshead Grammar School was founded in 1585 by Archbishop Sandys and later gained a fine reputation. William was educated there from 1779 to 1787. The two photographs show the school building in the late nineteenth century. As can be seen the building has been altered several times since the poet's days there.

The above picture shows the Grammar School almost as it is today. Below can be seen part of the schoolroom, where William first met contemporary poetry through the teachings of schoolmasters William Taylor and later James Bowman.

Two early photographs of the interior of Hawkshead School. On leaving, William wrote:

> Dear native regions, I foretell,
> From what I feel at this farewell,
> That, wheresoe'er my steps may tend,
> And whensoe'er my course shall end,
> If in that hour a single tie
> Survive of local sympathy,
> My soul will cast the backward view,
> The longing look alone on you.

William regularly walked the banks of Esthwaite Water. In later life he wrote of his experiences in 'An Evening Walk':

> Sweet are the sounds that mingle from afar,
> Heard by calm lakes, as peeps the folding star.
> Where the duck dabbles 'mid the rustling sedge,
> And feeding pike starts from the water's edge,
> Or the swan stirs the reeds, his neck and bill
> Wetting, that drip upon the water still;
> And heron, as resounds the trodden shore,
> Shoots upward, darting his long neck before.

After witnessing, on 18 June 1779, the recovery of the body of James Jackson, drowned in Esthwaite Water, he wrote:

> While from a boat others hung o'er the deep,
> Sounding with grappling irons and long poles.
> At last the dead man, 'mid that beauteous scene
> Of trees and hills and water, bolt upright
> Rose, with his ghastly face, a spectre shape
> Of terror . . .

Flag Street, Hawkshead, in an early photograph. The inhabitants drew their water from the stream below the street, seen here as William would have recognised it.

William and his elder brother Richard took lodgings with Hugh and Ann Tyson at their Hawkshead cottage in 1779. This became his second home and he remained part of the Tyson family until their deaths. In her latter years as a widow, Ann probably moved with William to Colthouse where William continued to visit her even after leaving Hawkshead school. Both this drawing and the photograph opposite were produced in the late nineteenth century.

Ye lowly cottages wherein we dwelt,
A ministration of your own was yours;
A sanctity, a safeguard and a love!
Can I forget you, being as you were
So beautiful among the pleasant fields
In which ye stood? Or can I here forget
The plain and seemly countenance with which
Ye dealt out your plain comforts? Yet had ye
Delights and exultations of your own.
Eager and never weary we pursued
Our home-amusements by the warm peat-fire
At evening, when with pencil, and smooth slate,
In square divisions parcelled out and all
With crosses and with cyphers scribbled o'er,
We schemed and puzzled, head opposed to head
In strife too humble to be named in verse:
Or round the naked table, snow-white deal,
Cherry or maple, sate in close array,
And to the combat, Loo or Whist, led on
A thick-ribbed Army; . . .

Hawkshead: three scenes in this quaint market town as William would have known it, although changes were taking place in his time. In 'The Prelude' he wrote:

A tranquillising spirit presses now
On my corporeal frame, so wide appears
The vacancy between me and those days
Which yet have such self-presence in my mind,
That, musing on them often do I seem
Two consciousnesses, conscious of myself
And of some other Being. A rude mass
Of native rock, left midway in the square
Of our small market village, was the goal
Or centre of these sports; and when, returned
After long absence, thither I repaired,
Gone was the old grey stone, and in its place
A smart Assembly-room usurped the ground
That had been ours. There let the fiddle scream,
And be ye happy! Yet, my Friends! I know
That more than one of you will think with me
Of those soft starry nights, and that old Dame
From whom the stone was named, who there had sate,
And watched her table with its huckster's wares
Assiduous, through the length of sixty years.

Richard Wordsworth, the poet's grandfather, was the first of the name who came to Westmorland. It was he who established a link with the Lowther estate that continued into William's time. Richard and his wife, Mary, lived at Sockbridge House in the parish of Barton, Westmorland (see p. 2). The two photographs show Barton church, often visited by William and Dorothy. It has been suggested that the famous daffodils were seen on one such pilgrimage on foot from Grasmere.

HOMES AT
GRASMERE & RYDAL

Reproductions of paintings of Dorothy Wordsworth,
William's sister, also appeared on early postcards.

A narrow girdle of rough stones and crags,
A rude and natural causeway, interposed
Between the water and a winding slope
Of copse and thicket, leaves the eastern shore
Of Grasmere safe in its own privacy. . . .

William and Dorothy came to this cottage at Town End, Grasmere, in December 1799. It was earlier an inn, the Dove and Olive Branch, and was later known as Dove Cottage. The above illustration is from a post card reproduction of a watercolour of the cottage in about 1805. The lower photograph was taken early this century by Abrahams of Keswick.

Herbert Bell, the Ambleside chemist (1856–1946), opened a photographic studio in the 1890s. He was a pillar of Lakeland society and a friend of Canon H.D. Rawnsley, Albert Fleming and Mary Armitt, among other members of the Ruskin Society who met in his studio. He was a founder member of the Armitt Library and librarian from 1912 to 1946. He was also a member of the Dove Cottage Committee, which started the present Wordsworth Museum. A large portion of his photographic archive is now held by the Armitt Library and Museum at Ambleside.

Among Herbert Bell's works is a series of photographs he took in and around Dove Cottage at the time it was acquired for the nation in 1890. He included in some of these pictures (pp. 24 and 30, and above) the Revd Stopford Brooke, whose initiative with Professor William Knight brought about the happy state of affairs we have today.

Three of Herbert Bell's photographs show the interior of Dove Cottage after it had become a museum. Thomas De Quincey occupied the cottage after the Wordsworths, holding the tenancy for twenty-eight years. He describes the main room in the cottage seen on the two photographs: 'It was an oblong square, not above eight and a half feet high, sixteen feet long and twelve feet broad, wainscoted from floor to ceiling with dark polished oak, slightly embellished with carving.'

Herbert Bell's view of the landing, staircase and back door of Dove Cottage.

The Abraham brothers of Keswick were among others who recorded the interior of Dove Cottage. These photographs show the ground-floor main room (above) and the 'parlour' (below). Prominent are the fireplaces. In his biography of Wordsworth Hunter Davies tells of William's description of the fire in his bedroom: 'the chimney draws perfectly and does not smoke at the first lighting of the fire.'

Dorothy's bedroom was entered directly from the porch at the front door. This is another Abraham photograph.

For at the bottom of the brow,
Where once the Dove and Olive-Bough
Offered a greeting of good ale
To all who entered Grasmere Vale;
And called on him who must depart
To leave it with a jovial heart;
There, where the Dove and Olive-Bough
Once hung, a Poet harbours now,
A simple water-drinking bard;
Why need our Hero then (though frail
His best resolves) be on his guard?

from 'The Waggoner'

Herbert Bell records the garden at Dove Cottage. William, anticipating leaving in 1802 on his marriage to
Mary Hutchinson of Penrith, wrote:

> Farewell, thou little Nook of mountain-ground,
> Thou rocky corner in the lowest stair
> Of that magnificent temple which doth bound
> One side of our whole vale with grandeur rare;
> Sweet garden-orchard, eminently fair,
> The loveliest spot that man hath ever found,
> Farewell! – we leave thee to Heaven's peaceful care,
> Thee, and the Cottage which thou dost surround.

from 'A Farewell'

Dorothy, Mary and William were assisted in constructing their garden by their neighbours, John and Agnes Fisher. John's sister, Molly, a much-loved simple girl, was their domestic servant.

Whose grateful owner can attest these truths
Even were the object nearer to our sight,
Would seem in no distinction to surpass
The rudest habitations. Ye might think
That it had sprung self-raised from earth, or grown
Out of the living rock, to be adorn'd
By nature only; but, if thither led,
Ye would discover, then, a studious work
Of many fancies prompting many hands,

Brought from the woods, the honeysuckle twines
Around the porch, in that trim place,
A plant no longer wild; the cultured rose
There blossoms, strong in health, and will be soon
Roof-high; the wild pink crowns the garden wall
And with the flowers are intermingled stones
Sparry and bright, the scatterings of the hills,
These ornaments that fade not with the year,
A hardy girl continues to provide. . . .

from 'The Abode'

Dorothy's early wish on arriving at Dove Cottage was for a shelter at the top of the back garden. First, in 1802, a bower was built and later, in 1804, a moss-lined summer house: 'A sort of larger Bird's nest (for it is lined with moss)', wrote Dorothy. Herbert Bell recorded their later replacements as De Quincey removed the originals on his occupancy of the cottage following the Wordsworths.

Allan Bank, deplored by William as an 'abomination' when it was built in 1805, was occupied by the Wordsworths, then a family with four children, from 1808 to 1811. The house has since been much altered and is currently owned by the National Trust. (This photograph is from the Dove Cottage collection)

The Parsonage opposite Grasmere church where the Wordsworth family lived from 1811 to 1813. They were not happy at either home; two children, Catherine and Thomas, died at the Parsonage.

On 1 May 1813 the Wordsworths moved to rent William's final home, Rydal Mount. The owner was Lady Le Fleming of nearby Rydal Hall. The drive to the Hall where it leaves the main road is shown in these two photographs, the first of which dates from the 1860s. The lower view from the 1930s shows how little the scene has changed.

Rydal Village showing Nab Scar.

Rydal church was opened at Christmas 1824. With advice on its siting by William, it is said to have cost Lady Le Fleming £1,500 to build. During its construction, he wrote:

> All who, around the hallowed Fane,
> Shall sojourn in the fair domain;
> Grateful to Thee, while service pure;
> And ancient ordinance, shall endure,
> For opportunity bestowed
> To kneel together, and adore their God!

The 'Thee' refers to Lady Diana Le Fleming.

Herbert Bell shows the interior of Rydal church following the alterations in the 1880s. Wordsworth is quoted as complaining in 1824: 'It has no chancel; the altar is unbecomingly confined; the pews are so narrow as to preclude the possibility of kneeling in comfort; there is no vestry; and what ought to have been first mentioned, the font, instead of standing at its proper place at the entrance, is thrust into the farther end of a pew.'

Above, we see Rydal Mount as it was in Wordsworth's day and below as altered in the later nineteenth century. It became a place of pilgrimage during his lifetime, and he enjoyed entertaining visitors in the garden.

Herbert Bell photographed the gate entrance to Rydal Mount in the snow before 1900.

Herbert Bell again shows Rydal Mount in the snow. In 1826 William wrote of his garden here:

The massy Ways, carried across these heights
By Roman perseverance, are destroyed,
Or hidden under ground, like sleeping worms.
How venture then to hope that Time will spare
This humble Walk? Yet on the mountain's side
A Poet's hand first shaped it; and the steps
Of that same Bard – repeated to and fro
At morn, at noon, and under moonlight skies
Through the vicissitudes of many a year –
Forbade the weeds to creep o'er its grey line.
No longer, scattering to the heedless winds
The vocal raptures of fresh poesy,
Shall he frequent these precincts; locked no more
In earnest converse with belovèd Friends,
Here will he gather stores of ready bliss,
As from the beds and borders of a garden
Choice flowers are gathered! But, if Power may spring
Out of a farewell yearning – favoured more
Than kindred wishes mated suitably
With vain regrets – the Exile would consign
This Walk, his loved possession, to the care
Of those pure Minds that reverence the Muse.

Herbert Bell returned to Rydal Mount in summer and again pictured the entrance gate, to contrast with the winter scene on p. 39. The entry in the 1885 *Bulmer's Guide to Westmorland* reads: 'Rydal Mount is a plain two-storey building, whose chief attraction is its association with the poet. It is now the residence of Robert Crewdson Esq., but it contains no relics of the poet, and the present occupant declines the intrusion of tourists.' In Kelly's *Directory* of 1897 the entry 'is now occupied by Robert Crewdson' seems to indicate there is nothing more to be said, but in 1905 the new Bulmer's *Directory* says: 'The house stands in artistically laid out grounds, planted with hollies by the poet. It is now the property and residence of J. Fisher Wordsworth Esq. J.P.'

Two views of the garden of Rydal Mount. 'Wordsworth's favourite long walk' is the title given to the postcard above. A visitor in 1833 recorded how 'He led me out into his garden and showed me the gravel walk in which thousands of his lines were composed.' The picture below is by Herbert Bell, who was probably glad to be able to gain entry in view of Robert Crewdson's policy. One of Herbert Bell's many projects was gaining entry to the poet's houses and haunts for Wordsworth lovers. His work in this cause, to produce today's happy situation, will probably never be fully known.

Before his death the poet is said to have loved showing parties of tourists round his grounds at Rydal Mount. In spite of Mr Crewdson's policy in the 1880s the popularity did not lessen, and a party of tourists on at least five charabanc coaches are here seen on such a visit at the turn of the century. Canon H.D. Rawnsley described the house as 'the haunt of the muses' and tells of how 'Backhouse, Mr Wordsworth's man i' th' house' used to creep along with his stick to Pelter Bridge and back. 'He used to break plates, you know, at his master's study door, so the saying is, for Mr Wordsworth was that deaf in his study.' Old Backhouse retained, after the poet's death, the stable lantern used by William and Dorothy on their nocturnal excursions from Rydal Mount. He was proud of the lantern, 'and no wonder either for Mr Wordsworth, so the saying is, did a deal of his poetry after dark'.

Nab Cottage looks on to Rydal Water on the road between Grasmere and Rydal. Hunter Davies recalls in his Wordsworth biography how Thomas De Quincey, friend of the Wordsworths, took up with a servant girl, daughter of the farmer who lived at Nab Cottage. Margaret produced a child in 1816, much to the disgust of the Wordsworth family. Later De Quincey purchased the property and held it until 1833. In 1849 Hartley Coleridge died there in an upstairs rented room.

Samuel Taylor Coleridge was a friend of the Wordsworths for many years, and as a drug addict caused them much anxiety. He lived for a time with the Wordsworths at Dove Cottage and with Robert Southey at Keswick. He died in 1834.

S.T. Coleridge's son, Hartley (1796–1849), showed literary brilliance as a child. After Hartley's death Wordsworth went with Derwent, Hartley's brother, to Grasmere church, to choose the site for his grave, next to Sarah Hutchinson's and near to Dora Wordsworth's. Hunter Davies records that William also reserved the site for his own and his wife's graves. 'Keep the ground for us, we are old people and it cannot be long.'

Hartley Coleridge

This drawing of Hartley Coleridge as a boy can also be found on early postcards.

William's landlady at Rydal Mount, Lady Le Fleming, decided to evict the Wordsworths in order to house her aunt. William averted this by purchasing the field known as Dora's Field, below Rydal Mount, and threatening to build a house.

The display of daffodils each year attracts many admirers. After his tenancy of Rydal Mount was assured, William drained the field and built a terrace next to the Mount. He then gave the field to his beloved daughter, Dora, hence the name.

Below Dora's Field we see Rydal Water. S.T. Coleridge describes this island as: 'A long round-pointed wedge of black glossy calm rocky island across the narrow, like the fragment of some huge bridge now overgrown with moss and trees.'

Rydal Water, described by both William and Dorothy, was much loved by the Wordsworth family. Both enjoyed skating on the lake, which was frequently frozen in the harsher winters of those days. The photograph below was taken in 1909.

Proud and exulting like an untired horse
That cares not for its home. All shod with steel,
We hissed along the polished ice in games
Confederate, imitative of the chase . . .

Grasmere from Red Bank. Dorothy, in her diary entry for 27 December 1801, wrote that the mere was 'a beautiful image of stillness, clear as glass, reflecting all things'.

The Vale of Rydal, photographed only eleven years after the poet's death by H. Bowness of Ambleside. The church is seen as it was originally built in 1824.

White Moss is the stretch of land between Rydal Water and Grasmere Lake. William described beggars who lived in the adjacent quarry. Dorothy also wrote of the same beggars in her *Journal*. It is from this quarry that the original main route left for Grasmere village, passing by Dove Cottage. The present main road was built in the 1830s, much to William's horror.

William's and Dorothy's favourite walk whilst at Dove Cottage took them into Easdale. Dorothy described the scene shown above in her *Journal*: 'A valley of streams and islands with that great waterfall at the head and lesser falls in different parts of the mountains, coming down to these rivers.' The early photograph below shows a shepherd with his flock in the same valley.

Artist Alfred Pettitt came to the Lake District in 1851 and opened an artist's studio at Grasmere in 1853. He there met William Baldry, a former Grasmere schoolmaster, and together they introduced commercial photography to the Lake District. In 1858 Alfred Pettitt moved to Keswick with his brother, and there they influenced the Abraham brothers and the Mayson family. The scene shown to the left is an early photograph of the Wordsworth Seat at Rydal by Pettitt and below is another view of it, by Herbert Bell of Ambleside, one of the next generation of Lakeland photographers.

The rock overlooking Rydal Water became very popular as tourism grew in the late nineteenth century and early this century. This view is from a contemporary postcard. What would the poet think today, when visiting the site is so difficult because of all the traffic?

The wishing gate, on the road from White Moss to Grasmere (the old main road into Grasmere via Town Head and Dove Cottage), can be seen here in two versions. In the *carte-de-visite* by R.J. Sproat of Grasmere from about 1870 (left) possibly the original gate can be seen; below is the replacement gate, as seen in about 1912. Guidebooks lavish praise on the view of the lake at Grasmere from this spot. Wordsworth wrote:

> The Worldling, pining to be freed
> From turmoil, who would turn or speed
> The current of his fate,
> Might stop before this favoured scene
> At Nature's call, nor blush to lean
> Upon the Wishing Gate.

The Prince of Wales Hotel was built in 1843 on the open land between Grasmere Lake and Dove Cottage by William Pearson, who was at Hawkshead School at the same time as William Wordsworth. Wordsworth was so annoyed that he disparaged the builder in his poetry.

Herbert Bell captures the rural atmosphere in his picture of ploughing overlooking the Rydal valley.

Wordsworth Harrison.

Canon H.D. Rawnsley, in his foreword to *Some Records of the Annual Grasmere Sports*, compiled in 1911 by Hugh Machell, says:

'Meanwhile here at Grasmere from far off times whereof man's memory runneth not to the contrary, wrestling had taken place always on the village green, or in the field near the Red Lion on the evening of Rushbearing Day, and thirty years ago I talked with an old man who remembered how sixty years before, Wordsworth had been present at the Grasmere wrestling and expressed his approval at the prowess of my informant.'

There is no doubt of the antiquity of the wrestling and racing around Grasmere, but it was not until 1852 that a small committee, John Pedder, John Harrison and Wordsworth Harrison, started the modern Grasmere Sports in the field adjoining the Red Lion. Wordsworth Harrison, whose mother was the poet's cousin, can be seen in the photograph opposite. Above, in a picture by William Baldry (see p. 52) we see an early Grasmere Sports. Baldry was the official photographer to the Sports for many years.

Two further pictures by William Baldry of early Grasmere Sports show the 'Foot Entrance' to the Sports field (above) and pole-leaping in 1876.

> The simple pastimes of the day and place
> By the fleet racers, ere the sun be set,
> The turf of yon large pasture will be skimm'd;
> There, too, the lusty wrestlers will contend;
> But know we not that he who intermits
> Th' appointed task and duties of the day,
> Untunes full off the pleasures of the day,
> Checking the finer spirits that refuse
> To flow when purposes are lightly changed?

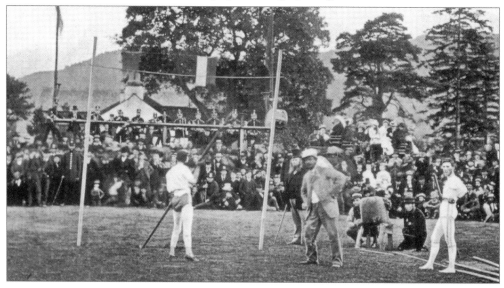

St Oswald's church at Grasmere was described in Book V of *The Excursion*:

> Not raised in nice proportions was the pile,
> But large and massy; for duration built;
> With pillars crowded, and the roof upheld
> By naked rafters intricately crossed,
> Like leafless underboughs in some thick wood,
> All withered by the depth of shade above.

The churchyard at Grasmere was where the Wordsworth children played. Catherine was there on the day she died in 1812. Graves there now include many of the Wordsworth family and friends.

Not William and Dora but a generation later; William's son Willy (1810–83) is seen here in a photograph from the 1860s with his daughter Mary Louisa (1849–1926). Willy succeeded his father as Comptroller of Stamps at Ambleside (see pp. 66–8).

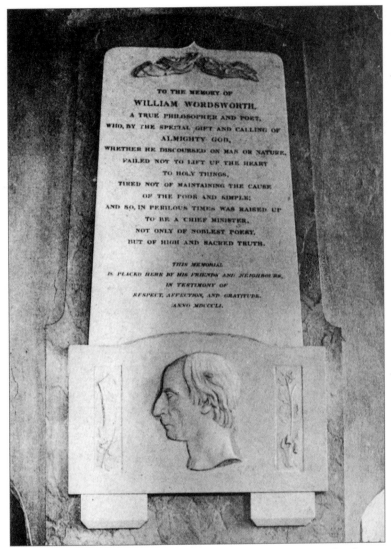

The William Wordsworth memorial in Grasmere church. William had written of such memorials in this church in Book V of *The Excursion*:

> Admonitory texts inscribed the walls,
> Each in its ornamental scroll enclosed;
> Each also crowned with winged heads – a pair
> Of rudely painted Cherubim. . . .
>
> And marble monuments were here displayed
> Thronging the walls. . . .
>
> The tribute by these various records claimed,
> Duly we paid, each after each, and read
> The ordinary chronicle of birth,
> Office, alliance, and promotion – all
> Ending in dust. . . .

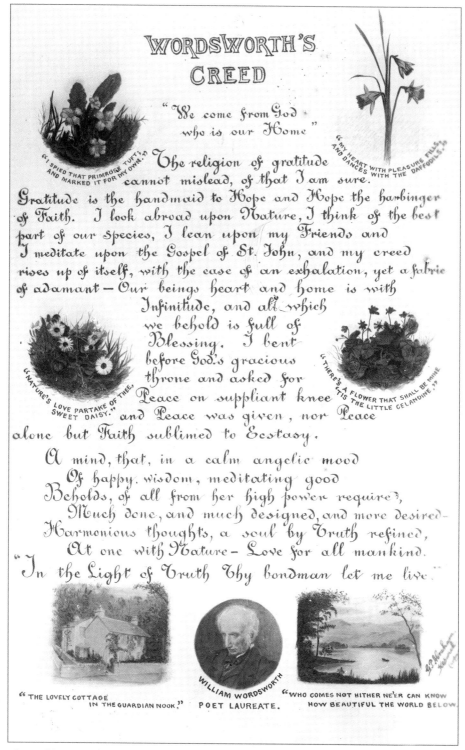

WORDSWORTH'S CREED

"We come from God who is our Home"

"I SPIED THAT PRIMROSE TUFT, AND MARKED IT FOR MY OWN."

"MY HEART WITH PLEASURE FILLS AND DANCES WITH THE DAFFODILS."

The religion of gratitude cannot mislead, of that I am sure. Gratitude is the handmaid to Hope and Hope the harbinger of Faith. I look abroad upon Nature, I think of the best part of our species, I lean upon my Friends and I meditate upon the Gospel of St. John, and my creed rises up of itself, with the ease of an exhalation, yet a fabric of adamant—Our beings heart and home is with Infinitude, and all which we behold is full of Blessing. I bent before God's gracious throne and asked for Peace on suppliant knee and Peace was given, nor Peace alone but Faith sublimed to Ecstasy.

"NATURE'S LOVE PARTAKE OF THEE, SWEET DAISY."

"THERE'S A FLOWER THAT SHALL BE MINE, 'TIS THE LITTLE CELANDINE."

A mind, that, in a calm angelic mood
Of happy wisdom, meditating good
Beholds, of all from her high power required,
Much done, and much designed, and more desired—
Harmonious thoughts, a soul by Truth refined,
At one with Nature—Love for all mankind.
"In the Light of Truth Thy bondman let me live."

"THE LOVELY COTTAGE IN THE GUARDIAN NOOK."

WILLIAM WORDSWORTH
POET LAUREATE.

"WHO COMES NOT HITHER NE'ER CAN KNOW HOW BEAUTIFUL THE WORLD BELOW."

'Wordsworth's Creed', as compiled by Keswick photographer G.P. Abraham, and sold to tourists on holiday postcards.

AMBLESIDE & WINDERMERE

*Portrait of Wordsworth (1844) by the American artist Henry Inman,
said by Mrs Wordsworth to be 'the best likeness that has been taken of him'.*

Herbert Bell's picture illustrates the nature of the roads round Ambleside not long after the poet's death. The turnpike roads of Wordsworth's days were taken over by the Quarter Sessions and then the new County Council in the 1880s. They remained unmade, dusty in summer and muddy in winter, for many decades after. The workman with his trousers tied with string and clogs may well have been a tramp as there were many on the roads in the latter part of the nineteenth century.

The origin of this photograph of the friends of William Wordsworth has yet to be clarified. It appears to date from the infancy of photography (1850–60) and yet it is included in the Bell lantern slides collection in the Herbert Bell collection. Herbert was not born until 1856 (six years after Wordsworth's death), so it seems likely that the picture was taken by one of a number of very early photographers in the Ambleside area and preserved for posterity by him. This is quite likely; his use of photography as a conservation tool can be seen in a number of places in this book. The four men pictured are said to be Dr James Shepherd, surgeon, the Revd Mr Tatham, Mr Smith and Dr William Fell, surgeon. The Armitt Library Bell collection includes pictures of a number of Ambleside characters from the end of the nineteenth century.

STAMP-OFFICE.

RECEIVED the _____ 13 Day of *September* 1825 _____ the Sum of

One Pound Nineteen Shillings Two Pence

for Duty on Account of the Personal Estate within-mentioned.

£ 1 „ 19 „ 2

Registered _____   Comptrolled _____

Rates of Duty payable on Legacies, Annuities and Residues, of the Amount or Value of £20 or upwards, by Stat. 55th Geo. III. Cap. 184.

The Description of the Legatee, or Annuitant, *must be in the following Words of the Act.*	Out of Personal Estate only. If the Deceased died any Time *before*, or upon the 5th April, 1805.	Out of Real or Personal Estate. If the Deceased died *after* the 5th April, 1805.
To Children of the Deceased, and their Descendants, or to the Father or Mother, or any Lineal Ancestor of the Deceased.	*(no Legacy Duty)*	£1. — per Cent.
To Brothers and Sisters of the Deceased, and their Descendants	£2. 10s. per Cent	£3. — per Cent.
To Brothers and Sisters of the Father or Mother of the Deceased, and their Descendants.	£4. — per Cent.	£5. — per Cent.
To Brothers and Sisters of the Grandfather or Grandmother of the Deceased, and their Descendants	£5. — per Cent.	£6. — per Cent.
To any Person in any other Degree of Collateral Consanguinity, or to any Stranger in Blood, to the Deceased........	£8. — per Cent.	£10. — per Cent.

Where any Legatee shall take Two or more distinct Legacies or Benefits under any Will or Testamentary Instrument, which shall together be of the Amount or Value of £20 each shall be charged with Duty, although each or either may be separately under that Amount or Value.

The Husband or Wife of the Deceased is not chargeable with Duty.

Printed by J. Hartnell, Wine Office Court, Fleet Street, for His Majesty's Stationery Office.

The office of Distributor of Stamps (a tax collector) for Westmorland was described as 'the £400 sinecure' when it was held by William Wordsworth. Before he took the post Wordsworth did not realise that he had to pay a £100 a year pension from this sum to the previous Distributor. In the same year (1813) that he took the post his friend Robert Southey became the Poet Laureate. (It was not until 1843 that William became Laureate.) Hunter Davies writes of the financial problems of Wordsworth and of the string pulling he had to do to get a secure income. Above, and on the next page, we reproduce two documents from 1825, during Wordsworth's days as Distributor. In 1843, his income assured from other sources, he passed the job on to his son Willy who, up to then, had failed to secure any sort of position.

Form No. 1.

To be used from and after the 31st Day of August, 1815.

STAMP OFFICE.

Receipt and Discharge for any Specific, Pecuniary or other

LEGACY,

Given out of Personal Estate, or out of or charged upon Real Estate, or out of Monies arising by the Sale or Mortgage of Real Estate. and for the Residue, or any Share of Residue of Personal Estate, or the Residue, or any Share of Residue of Monies arising by the Sale or Mortgage of Real Estate, where the same shall be of the Amount or Value of £20 or upwards, and given or devolving to, or for the Benefit of any Child, or Descendant of any Child, or the Father or Mother or any lineal Ancestor, or to collateral Relations or Strangers in Blood to the Deceased, pursuant to Acts 36 Geo. 3. Cap. 52.—45 Geo. 3. Cap. 28. and 55 Geo. 3. Cap. 184.

Administration Register *A.I*_____ N.º *1*_____ 182*5*___ Folio. *131.*

On Account of the Personal (^) _____ Estate of *Margaret Hart* late of *Ireleth in the Parish of Dalton in the County of Lancaster Spinster* who died on the _____ Day of _____ One Thousand Eight Hundred and *twenty five*

Between

Names of the Executors or Administrators, Devisees in Trust, or Heir at Law.	Their Residence.	and Profession.	State whether Executors, Administrators, Devisees in Trust, or Heir at Law.
Ellen Robinson the Wife of John Robinson of Oaks Park in the Parish of Colton in the said County		*Gentleman*	*Administratrix*

Acting under ~~Probate of Will, or~~ Letters of Administration, granted by the *Consistory* _____ Court of *Richmond Rep̄ab at Lancaster* on the *13th* Day of *June* _____ One Thousand Eight Hundred and *twenty five*

And

Name of the Legatee or next of Kin.	Degree of Relationship, if any, to be here stated as on the other Side.	Describe the Nature of the Bequest, and if Residue, say what Part or Share.	Price of Stocks.	Value.	Rate of Duty per Cent.	Amount of Duty.
William Hart	*a Descendant of a Brother of the deceased*	*One third of the Residue*		£ *65* s *15* d *6½*	*3*	£ *1* s *19* d *5* / *18.10*

(*) _____

£71. 6. 7½

(^c) **Received** _____ the *sixth* Day of *September* 182*6* the Sum of *Sixty five pounds fifteen shillings and six pence* _____ being *my one third* _____ ~~Legacy or~~ _____ Share of Residue out of the Personal (^c) _____ Estate above mentioned, having first allowed or paid *one pound nineteen shillings and five pence* _____ for the Duty thereon.

Witness Tho.ˢ Parkinson _____ *W H, W Hart*

(^) If a Legacy be satisfied out of Real Estate, the Word *Real* must be substituted for *Personal.*

(^B) In Cases of Legacies given in Trust for Infants, then state in the Space above "in Trust for the said Legatee a Minor," or if given to be enjoyed by different Persons in Succession, all chargeable with the *same* Rate of Duty, or subjected to any Contingency, or Power of Appointment, or bequeathed in any other special Manner to, or for more than one Person, then state the Particulars of such Bequest.

(^c) If the Legacy be "*Retained in Trust,*" substitute those Words for the Word "*Received.*"

On Legacies given in Succession, to Persons chargeable with *different* Rates of Duty, the Persons entitled for Life only, are to pay Duty as Annuitants, and must therefore give their Receipts in the Form to be used for Annuities No. 2.

In Cases of Residues or Shares of Residues of Personal Estate, retained by Executors or Administrators, either to their own Use, as Residuary Legatees or next of Kin, or as Trustees for the Use and Benefit of others, and in Cases of Residues, or Shares of Residues of Monies arising from Real Estate, retained by Executors or Trustees in like Manner, a particular Account must be given of the Property according to a printed Form No. 3, provided for the Purpose, and to be had at the Stamp Office, or of the Distributers of Stamps.

PENALTIES.

The *Receipt* must be dated on the Day of signing, and the Duty paid within 21 Days after, under a Penalty of £10 per Cent. on the amount of the Duty, *and if the Duty is not paid within Three Months from the Date of the Receipt, a Penalty will be incurred of £10 per Cent. on the amount or value of the Legacy.*

Opposite the Royal Oak Inn in Ambleside was the old stamp office, in which Wordsworth carried on his collection of stamp tax on legal documents. It was not, as many think, a post office, but a tax office. The modern Ambleside post office occupies a site in the Market Place, which was the home of William Green (1760–1823), an artist who was a friend of, and much admired by, William Wordsworth and his circle of friends. William Green is buried in Grasmere churchyard, where his epitaph can be seen; it was written by Wordsworth. At the Armitt Library in Ambleside can be seen some of Green's original work.

Two views of old Ambleside show (right) the famous Bridge House in its original state, as photographed by R.J. Sproat of Grasmere in the 1860s, and (below) the Windermere to Keswick Turnpike toll booth at Waterhead, photographed by Herbert Bell of Ambleside before the take-over of the roads in the 1880s by Quarter Sessions and then the County Council. Wordsworth knew both places and would certainly recognise the Bridge House today, even through its necklace of motor vehicles; one can but wonder, though, what he would think of the modern use of the toll booth site!

These two nineteenth-century views of the head of Windermere at Waterhead, Ambleside, show scenes that Wordsworth would have recognised. In the top view, the rural tranquillity that William would have known at Waterhead for most of his life has hardly changed but below, where the road to Langdale and Coniston left the turnpike road, the busy boatyard and the small hotel indicate the start of the modern commercialised resort.

The old mill at Ambleside is on the Stockghyll where the stream runs through the town. 'Before you leave Ambleside give three minutes to looking at a passage of the brook which runs through the town; it is to be seen from a garden on the right bank of the stream a few steps above the bridge – Stockgill Force, upon the stream, will have been mentioned to you as one of the sights of the neighbourhood,' says Wordsworth's *Guide to the Lakes*.

Two scenes on Dorothy Wordsworth's favourite route home to Rydal from Ambleside. In the top picture can be seen the bridge over the Rothay with the spire of Ambleside's St Mary's church of 1854 (see pp. 156–7) in the background. An early photographer adjusts his plate camera. In the picture below are the stepping stones under Loughrigg. Dorothy called this route Clappersgate, taking her name no doubt from the large slates called clappers that form field and road boundaries hereabouts.

As a child Harriet Martineau was an admirer of
Wordsworth, and that attraction took her in
1843, in middle age, to buy a plot of land at
Ambleside on which to build a house. She
became quite friendly with William, who
admired her intellect but was sceptical about
her politics and lifestyle. In 1846 she built The
Knoll and he helped her plant trees in the
garden and inscribe the sundial. After
Wordsworth's death she became an important
figure in Ambleside society in spite of her
eccentric way of life, which included
vegetarianism, mesmerism, experiments in
agriculture and atheism. She, like William,
wrote a *Guide to the Lakes*, and today she shares,
with others of her time, a place in the story of
Ambleside at the Armitt Library. In the lower
picture the front of The Knoll is recorded by
Herbert Bell, another Armitt Library worthy.

Wordsworth encouraged the headmaster of Rugby School, Dr Thomas Arnold (below), to buy a plot of land on the under Loughrigg road from Ambleside to Rydal. On the land Dr Arnold built Fox How as a holiday home in 1833. Wordsworth is said to have advised on the architectural style of the house and he even mentions it, in passing, in his *Guide to the Lakes*. Dr Arnold died in 1842, eight years before Wordsworth, but his family continued to own the house for some decades after. It is of interest that Wordsworth, fierce protector of the Lake District, should also encourage such development. Fox How attracted attention in both artistic reproduction (above) and photograph (opposite, above).

'Dr Arnold (of Rugby)' is the title of this early Abraham Brothers of Keswick postcard.

In 1820, when Thomas de Quincey found Dove Cottage too small for his family, he sought accommodation elsewhere (as had the Wordsworths before), and it was to Fox Ghyll (above) that he came. Situated on Dorothy's Clappersgate route from Ambleside to Rydal, this too was part of the gentrified development that Wordsworth seemed to actively encourage. Nearby is Loughrigg Holme where Dora Wordsworth, William's daughter, and Edward Quillinan, her husband, came to live for a short time before her death.

Skelwith Bridge (above) and its saw and bobbin mill, run by the Coward family, are pictured at the turn of
the century. The picture below is by Herbert Bell of Ambleside, anxious as always to record such scenes
for posterity. The Coward family of High Furness (related to one of the authors) is typical of those
described by Wordsworth in his *Guide to the Lakes* — peasants who had to look to other things during the
lifetime of the poet (see p. 152). The ones who went into wood-turning by waterpower became involved
in John Ruskin's attempt to re-establish 'home industry' in the small farms of the Lakes, when they made
spinning wheels from home industry patterns that had died out over fifty years before.

'Tarns are found in some of the vales, and are numerous upon the mountains' says Wordsworth's *Guide*. 'A Tarn, in a vale, implies, for the most part, that the bed of the vale is not happily formed; that the water of the brooks can neither wholly escape, nor diffuse itself over a larger area. Accordingly, in such situations, Tarns are often surrounded by an unsightly tract of boggy ground – [the tarn] differs only from the Lake in being smaller, and in belonging mostly to a smaller valley or circular recess.'

Above we see Elterwater and below Little Langdale Tarn with Wetherlam behind.

Three pictures in the Langdales show Dungeon Ghyll waterfall, Mickleden and nineteenth-century tourists descending from Wrynose Pass. The photographs shown left and below left are by Herbert Bell of Ambleside.

> It was a spot which you may see
> If ever you to Langdale go,
> Into a chasm a mighty block
> Hath fallen, and made a bridge of rock:
> The gulf is deep below;
> And, in a basin black and small,
> Receives a lofty waterfall.

A Riggs of Windermere charabanc coach is pictured after an accident on the Blea Tarn road between Little and Great Langdale, *c.* 1900. Herbert Bell, a passenger, was able to take some unexpected pictures. One lady in the foreground of the picture seems to be injured and behind an obviously shaken coachman is sitting recovering from the ordeal. Correct as ever, he has kept his Riggs' top hat in place! Coaching accidents were many and most were reported in the local press. In his *A coach drive at the Lakes* of 1890 Canon H.D. Rawnsley describes an incident involving the Whitehaven mail coach:

'Just before reaching Rougha or Rough Howe Bridge, had we been here on a certain day nigh fifty years ago, we should have seen the Whitehaven Mail come round the corner, crash into a pony-chaise with two middle aged men in it, have seen the pony-chaise, occupants and all, fly over – or rather through – the wall, and heard one of the gentlemen pick himself up and say, in a solemn way, "I shall have this matter thoroughly investigated." We should have heard David Johnson, the driver – pale as death, and pulling up sharp and looking over his shoulder – say, "Good God! it's Maister Wadswuth." And, had we been in Keswick market-place that night, and asked whether Mr Wordsworth was much hurt, we should have heard David say, "No, sir, thank Heaven for that sir! But I never heard a body's tongue swear, gladlier though, for I thowt we'd kilt the poit." As confirming the story, the writer may mention that he was driving by the spot the other day with the Archbishop of York, and mentioned the incident. "Dear me," said his Grace, "You recall a drive I had years ago with the very driver of the identical coach. I was a lad coming from school, on my way to my home in Whitehaven, and here Johnson told me of the collision he had with Wordsworth's pony carriage, and of the anger of the poet, he further told me how the accident happened. It seems his off wheeler tossed his head and got the bit entangled in the pole hook; in consequence, Johnson lost control, and accident as they came down the incline was unavoidable."'

In his *Guide to the Lakes* Wordsworth invites tourists to visit Tilberthwaite.

'He beholds, rising apparently from its base, the cluster of mountains among which he is going to wander, and towards whose recesses, by the Vale of Coniston, he is gradually and peacefully led. From the Inn at the head of Coniston Lake, a leisurely Traveller might have much pleasure in looking into Yewdale and Tilberthwaite. . . . the beauty which gave the scene is much heightened by a single cottage, or cluster of cottages, that will almost always be found under these rocks and hills. . . . These dwellings, mostly built, as has been said, of rough unhewn stone, are roofed with slates, which were rudely taken from the quarry before the present art of splitting them was fully understood, and are, therefore, rough and uneven in their surface, so that both the coverings and sides of the houses have furnished places of rest for the seeds of lichen, mosses, ferns, and flowers. Hence buildings, which in their very form call to mind the processes of Nature, do thus, clothed in part with a vegetable garb, appear to be received into the bosom of the living principle of things, as it acts and exists among the woods and fields; and by their colour and their shape, affectingly direct the thoughts to that tranquil course of Nature and simplicity, along which the humble-minded inhabitants have, through many generations, been led.'

(See p. 88 for further comments on the Lakeland cottage.)

Windermere from above Lowood (above) and Windermere Bowness bay (below). Returning home from University, Wordsworth wrote:

Standing alone, as from a rampart's edge,
I overlooked the bed of Windermere,
Like a vast river, stretching in the sun.
With exultation, at my feet I saw
Lake, islands, promontories, gleaming bays,
A universe of Nature's fairest forms . . .

R. and W. Brunskill were nineteenth-century Windermere photographers and both these pictures of Bowness are from their studios. St Martin's church at Bowness, which Wordsworth would have known, was very much altered over three years from 1870. The picture above is from before the alterations. The top of Crag Brow with the huge chestnut tree, which appeals in 1906 did not save, would also have been known to the poet. William was disgusted at the alterations taking place in his lifetime. What would he think now?

The arrival of the railway at Birthwaite (later renamed Windermere) in 1847 caused an extension of the development that had been taking place in the Windermere area for the past fifty years. Wordsworth bought shares in the railway company, as he could see it was a good investment, and also wrote a sonnet (see overleaf) condemning the event. Above can be seen the London & North Western railway station at Windermere (it is now a supermarket!) and below the Rigg's coach which took the tourist on to Keswick. There were plans to continue the railway through Ambleside and Grasmere to Keswick, but objectors (including Wordsworth) stopped them. The Rigg family owned the hotel opposite the station and also had their coaching offices in the station building.

Our Summer Quarters near Windermere

The Cynicus holiday postcards were overprinted with the name of the tourist resort. Just after fifty years following the poet's death the seeds sown in Father West's and Wordsworth's own guidebooks (which ran to many revised reprints to keep up to date with the changing scene) were coming to fruition, with thousands arriving in Lakeland on the railways and by road. In 1844, as the railways were being planned, the poet wrote this sonnet:

> Is then no nook of English ground secure
> From rash assault? Schemes of retirement sown
> In youth, and 'mid the busy world kept pure
> As when their earliest flowers of hope were blown,
> Must perish; – how can they this blight endure?
> And must he too the ruthless change bemoan
> Who scorns a false utilitarian lure
> 'Mid his paternal fields at random thrown?
> Baffle the threat, bright Scene, from Orrest-head
> Given to the pausing traveller's rapturous glance;
> Plead for thy peace, thou beautiful romance
> Of nature; and, if human hearts be dead,
> Speak, passing winds; ye torrents, with your strong
> And constant voice, protest against the wrong.

When the postcard above was sent, 'the bright Scene, from Orrest-head' was no longer 'given to the pausing traveller's rapturous glance', but was being observed by many thousands of holidaymakers, drawn by romantic descriptions and holiday trade advertising.

Wordsworth frequently crossed Windermere on the ferry, which is part of the medieval main road between the market towns of Kendal and Hawkshead. The ferry boat was in those days a rowing boat. In the top picture is the ferry boat house at Low Millerground, and in the bottom picture the ferrymen are loading horses, and possibly a cart, at Claife. In Wordsworth's poem 'An Evening Walk' we can read:

> Air listens like the sleeping water, still,
> To catch the spiritual music of the hill,
> Broke only by the slow clock tolling deep,
> Or shout that wakes the ferryman from sleep,
> The echoed hoof nearing the distant shore,
> The boat's first motion – made with dashing oar. . . .

The old Ferry Inn from where the ferry left to cross the lake to Bowness. The scene has much changed. The replacement Ferry Hotel of 1880 is now offices and a laboratory, and a busy road brings motorised traffic to a modern ferry boat.

Wray Castle was built by Liverpool surgeon James Dawson ten years before Wordsworth's death. William seemed to have no objection to the erection of this 'folly' type of house. He is said to have thought it 'dignified'. The Potter family came here on holiday in 1882, and it was then that Beatrix Potter met the local vicar, Canon H.D. Rawnsley, whom she was later to help found the National Trust.

When, on thy bosom, spacious Windermere!
A Youth, I practised this delightful art;
Tossed on the waves alone, or 'mid a crew
Of joyous comrades. Soon as the reedy marge
Was cleared I dipped, with arms accordant, oars
Free from obstruction; and the boat advanced
Through crystal water, smoothly as a hawk,
That, disentangled from the shady boughs
Of some thick wood, her place of covert, cleaves
With correspondent wings the abyss of air.

Hush, there is some one on the stir!
'Tis Benjamin the Waggoner;
Who long hath trod this toilsome way,
Companion of the night and day.
That far-off tinkling's drowsy cheer,
Mixed with a faint yet grating sound
In a moment lost and found. . . .
Many a stop and stay he makes,
Many a breathing-fit he takes;
Steep the way and wearisome,
Yet all the while his whip is dumb!
                    from 'The Waggoner'

In his *Guide* Wordsworth talks about the cottages to be seen in all parts of the district. The above, from Bowness on Windermere, is typical.

'The dwelling houses and contiguous outhouses, are, in many instances, of the colour of the native rock, out of which they have been built; but frequently the Dwelling or Fire-house, as it is ordinarily called, has been distinguished from the barn or byre by rough-cast and whitewash, which, as the inhabitants are not hasty in renewing it, in a few years acquires, by the influence of the weather, a tint at once sober and variegated. As these houses have been, from father to son, inhabited by persons engaged in the same occupations, yet necessarily with changes in the circumstances, they have received without incongruity additions and accommodations adopted to the needs of each successive occupant, who, being for the most part proprietor, was at liberty to follow his own fancy: so that these humble dwellings remind the contemplative spectator of a product of Nature, and may (using a strong expression) rather be said to have grown than to have been erected; to have risen, by an instinct of their own out of the native rock – so little is there in them of formality, such is their wildness and beauty.'

OVER KIRKSTONE TO THE DAFFODILS OF ULLSWATER

Wordsworth, an engraving after the painting by R. Carruthers.

'Windermere communicates with two lateral valleys,' reads Wordsworth's *Guide*, 'That of Troutbeck, distinguished by the mountains at its head – by picturesque remains of cottage architecture; and, towards the lower part by bold foregrounds formed by steep and winding banks of the river.' The Brownes' house in Troutbeck, always picturesque, was photographed at the turn of the century by Brunskills, early photographers of Windermere.

The summit of Kirkstone Pass on 3 August 1864, as photographed by J. Garnett of the Windermere post office. 'How beautiful the world below' wrote the poet.

In the picture above, the telegraph has arrived on Kirkstone summit, and below, Kendal photographer Joe Sawyer's wife poses at the front of the Inn. William wrote in an ode 'The Pass of Kirkstone':

This block – and yon, whose church-like frame
Gives to this savage Pass its name. . . .

'Many of the fragments of rock on the top and slopes of Kirkstone, and of similar places, are fantastic enough in themselves; but the full effect of such impressions can only be had in a state of weather when they are not likely to be sought for,' says Wordsworth's *Guide*, where he is describing a walking trip to Ullswater over the pass. He goes on to discuss the naming of Brothers Water, which can just be glimpsed in the top picture.

Canon H.D. Rawnsley quotes Scott and
Wordsworth in his *The Story of Gough and his
Dog on Helvellyn*. Scott's poem reads:

On the right, Striding Edge round the Red
    Tarn was bending,
And Catchedecam its left verge was defending,
One huge nameless rock in the front was
    impending. . . .

Wordsworth wrote:

It was a cove, a huge recess,
That keeps, till June December's snow;
A lofty precipice in front,
A silent tarn below!

Both Wordsworth and his friend Sir Walter Scott wrote of the death of Charles Gough on Helvellyn in 1805. The Kendal Quaker's body was guarded by his dog for some three months. Miss Frances Power Cobbe suggested to Canon Rawnsley, then at Crosthwaite, Keswick, that 'some record of that heroic creature should be placed where passers by might see and ponder'. Canon Rawnsley had a memorial erected on the spot. Two verses of Wordsworth's eight-verse ode 'Fidelity' were carved on to a slate which was built into a memorial in 1891. Herbert Bell, the Ambleside photographer, recorded the building of the monument in the top picture and Lowe, the Patterdale photographer, climbed the mountain not long after completion to show the finished memorial. The verses start as follows:

> The Dog, which still was hovering nigh,
> Repeating the same timid cry,
> This Dog had been through three months' space
> A dweller in that savage place.

It is doubtful if anything in this picture (by Lowe of Patterdale) of Deepdale and Fairfield has changed since the days of the poet. Both William and Dorothy would have known these fells well; in his *Guide* William says:

'Having retraced the banks of the stream to Patterdale, and pursued the road up the main Dale, the next considerable stream would, if ascended in the same manner [as the visit to Grisedale] conduct to Deepdale, the character of which Valley may be conjectured from its name. It is terminated by a cove, a craggy and gloomy abyss, with precipitous sides; a faithful receptacle of the snows that are driven into it, by the west wind, from the summit of Fairfield.'

The route from Patterdale to Grasmere via Grisedale is recorded by William in his *Guide*:

'At the head of the lake (we being now in Patterdale) we cross a fifth stream, Grisedale Beck: this would conduct through a woody steep, where may be seen some unusually large ancient hollies, up to the level area of the valley of Grisedale; hence there is a path for foot-travellers, and along which a horse may be led, to Grasmere. A sublime combination of mountain forms appears in front while ascending the bed of this valley, and the impression increases till the path leads almost immediately under the projecting masses of Helvellyn.'

Dorothy Wordsworth's *Journal* records travelling over this pass a number of times and includes the last time they saw John Wordsworth in the Lakes: 'On Monday 29th [September 1800] John left us, Wm & I parted with him in sight of Ullswater. It was a fine day, showery but with sunshine and fine clouds — I could not help thinking that we should see him again because he was only going to Penrith.' An inscription on a stone marks the point of their parting.

Scenes with cows gathered at the edge of Ullswater would have been familiar to the Wordsworths on their frequent excursions. He wrote of a similar group elsewhere:

> The cattle crowding round the beverage clear
> To slake their thirst with reckless hoofs have trod
> The encircling turf into a barren clod. . . .

Photographer Lowe of Patterdale, at his artistic best in his own area, took the pictures here and opposite. In the picture above is St Patrick's well by the road and lakeside, and below is the late nineteenth-century village centre nearby. Dorothy Wordsworth describes in her *Journal* an overnight stay she had with William at Dobson's boarding house in April 1802. 'When I undrew my curtains in the morning I was much affected by the beauty of the prospect.'

Patterdale Hall was rebuilt in what has been described as an Italianate style in 1796. Dorothy called it 'an offensive object'. This was the hall of the Mounsey family, 'Kings of Patterdale', who had lived on the site for several generations. The Wordsworths knew the Mounsey clan and their history. Dorothy was not pleased with the cruel 'King' who drove his wife to drink. John Marshall, a friend and frequent companion of the Wordsworths, married Jane Pollard, a close friend of Dorothy to whom Dorothy wrote letters that today reveal so much of her life. He bought the estate in 1824 and came to live in Patterdale Hall.

William's poem, 'Airey-force Valley' includes
the following lines:

. . . the brook itself,
Old as the hills that feed it from afar,
Doth rather deepen than disturb the calm
Where all things else are still and motionless.
And yet, even now, a little breeze, perchance
Escaped from boisterous winds that rage
    without,
Has entered, by the sturdy oaks unfelt. . . .

William's *Guide* says of the place where
Ullswater becomes the River Eamont: 'If
Ullswater be approached from Penrith, a mile
and a half brings you to the winding vale of
Eamont, and the prospects increase in interest
till you reach Patterdale; but the first four miles
along Ullswater by this road are comparatively
tame. . . .'

Turn-of-the-century photographer Lowe of Patterdale went along Ullswater side to photograph daffodils for his postcard customers.

On 15 April 1802 Dorothy Wordsworth recorded in her *Journal* a journey she took on foot with William into Gowbarrow Park, Ullswater:

'When we were in the woods beyond Gowbarrow Park we saw a few Daffodils close to the waterside, we fancied that the lake had floated the seeds ashore and that the little colony had so sprung up – But as we went along there were more and yet more, and at last under the boughs of the trees, we saw that there was a long belt of them along the shore, along the breadth of the county turnpike road. I never saw Daffodils so beautiful; they grew among the mossy stones about and about them, some resting their heads upon these stones as on a pillow for weariness and the rest tossed and reeled and danced and seemed as if they verily laughed with the wind that blew upon them over the Lake, they looked so gay ever glancing ever changing. There was here and there a little knott and a few stragglers a few yards higher up but there were so few as not to disturb the simplicity and unity and life of that one busy highway – we rested again and again.'

William transformed their experience into poetry a few years later:

> I wandered lonely as a cloud
> That floats on high o'er vales and hills,
> When all at once I saw a crowd,
> A host, of golden daffodils;
> Beside the lake, beneath the trees,
> Fluttering and dancing in the breeze.
>
> Continuous as the stars that shine
> And twinkle on the milky way,
> They stretched in never-ending line
> Along the margin of a bay:
> Ten thousand saw I at a glance,
> Tossing their heads in sprightly dance.
>
> The waves beside them danced; but they
> Out-did the sparkling waves in glee:
> A poet could not but be gay,
> In such a jocund company:
> I gazed – and gazed – but little thought
> What wealth the show to me had brought:
>
> For oft, when on my couch I lie
> In vacant or in pensive mood,
> They flash upon that inward eye
> Which is the bliss of solitude;
> And then my heart with pleasure fills,
> And dances with the daffodils.

KESWICK &
CENTRAL LAKELAND

*Robert Southey, from whose writings we know so much about
Wordsworth, was also included on postcard reproductions. He
died in 1843 and pictures of his grave in Crosthwaite
churchyard near Keswick were also sold to tourists (see p. 114).*

The church at Wythburn was opposite one of the village's two inns, the Nag's Head. It, like the Cherry Tree (opposite), was destroyed. The church survived the flooding by Manchester Corporation who paid for it to be improved. In Wordsworth's day it was a very poor building in bad repair. In 'The Waggoner' he describes it as 'Wytheburne's modest House of prayer / As lowly as the lowliest dwelling. . . .' It now stands in isolation near tree plantations, against a busy motor road looking out on to the waters of a reservoir.

Both photographs are by Alfred Pettitt, who had started his career in Ambleside a year after the poet's death, then later moved to Keswick.

The Cherry Tree Inn, on the old route, now flooded, through Wythburn, also features in that favourite poem of Wordsworth, 'The Waggoner'. He tells how Benjamin takes his wagon from Ambleside to Keswick and after managing to pass the inns in Grasmere was drenched in a storm. He then picks up a woman and her baby, her husband and an old sailor. They all come down into Wythburn and the cheerful sounds of the 'Merry-night' – the shepherds' (and others') get-together in the Cherry Tree Inn – greets them. The sailor and the waggoner go in and join in the festivities, and leave in an alcoholic haze:

> What tears of rapture, what vow-making,
> Profound entreaties, and hand-shaking!
> What solemn, vacant, interlacing,
> As if they'd fall asleep embracing!

The comings and goings to the Cherry Tree are hard to imagine in this photograph taken by Herbert Bell of Ambleside. Rupert Potter, father of the famous Beatrix, also photographed the Thirlmere area before the Manchester Corporation Water Engineers destroyed it for ever (see our *The Lake Counties of One Hundred Years Ago*). The Herbert Bell pictures are held at the Armitt Library in Ambleside, and part of the Rupert Potter archive is at the County Record Office in Kendal.

A nineteenth-century view of Thirlmere before the valley was flooded. The narrowing of the lake to where the bridges used to be (see pp. 108–9) can be seen. Wordsworth takes his readers to the best views in his *Guide*: 'Having previously enquired, at the Inn near Wythburn chapel, the best way from the sixth milestone from Keswick to the bridge that divides the Lake, he must cross it and proceed with the Lake on the right to the hamlet a little beyond its termination, and rejoin the road upon Shoulthwaite Moss, about four miles from Keswick.' The Raphael Tuck oilette postcard from the turn of the century (below) illustrates the route along the lake as the poet would have known it.

The Rock of Names stood on the old road that ran from Wythburn towards Keswick along the side of Thirlmere. It stood halfway between Grasmere and Keswick, where the Coleridges and the Wordsworths often met. The friends, the Wordsworths, Southey, Coleridge and Prof. Wilson, carved their names or initials on the flat surface of part of the rock. It got in the way of the water engineers in the 1890s and they blew it up. Canon Rawnsley is said to have reassembled some of the fragments in a cairn above the new road being constructed by the Manchester Corporation, and there they remained until they were removed in the 1980s for safe keeping to the Wordsworth Museum at Dove Cottage. The Lake District planners, strangely, demanded that the fragments be returned to the site where they had been from the 1890s and that is where they rest today, in a position completely ruined by tree plantation and motor traffic on the nearby main road. Herbert Bell of Ambleside, no doubt aware of the risk to the rock, photographed the Rock of Names in its original position, and his picture is shown above. To the right is the cairn jumble of fragments as Canon Rawnsley assembled them, photographed by the Abraham brothers of Keswick.

The bridges across the narrows dividing the lakes in Thirlmere valley were a feature until they too were lost to the reservoir. Herbert Bell recorded the scene just before the water engineers destroyed it. Wordsworth, in his *Guide to the Lakes*, takes his tourist (see p. 106) across this bridge – 'he must cross it' – and later talks about the risk that 'alluvial promontories' (such as this) 'Threaten in some places to bisect the waters which they have long adorned, and, in the course of some ages, they will cause some of the lakes to dwindle into numerous and insignificant pools, which in their turn will finally be filled up'. He could not have known that the opposite would take place just a few decades after his death, as his road from Grasmere to Keswick was flooded.

The old road along the lakeside from Wythburn can be seen on the right of this picture. This is the road the Wordsworths knew well and it is the route the Waggoner took in the poem. Although thirsty still, in spite of drinking at the Cherry Tree, Benjamin and his pals dare not refresh themselves from the lake, as,

Once in (I put the question plain)
Who is to help them out again?

The Stone Circle at Castlerigg (above) was just off the Wordsworths' route to Keswick. It is recorded that Wordsworth and his friend Samuel Taylor Coleridge visited it 200 years ago in 1799. Below, not one but two waggoners wend their slow way up the hill on the road to Grasmere from Keswick. They have just passed the toll bar, and would not be too concerned with the scene, of which Wordsworth said: 'I do not indeed know any tract of country in which, within so narrow a compass, may be found an equal variety in the influence on light and shadow upon the sublime or beautiful features of landscape. . . .'

The poet Percy Bysshe Shelley eloped in 1811 with his sixteen-year-old bride Harriet Westbrook. In November of that year they rented Chestnut Hill, Keswick (the sketch above is by A. Forestier), now called Shelley's Cottage. Shelley hoped to meet Southey and Wordsworth. Hunter Davies, in his biography of Wordsworth, tells how Shelley thought that Southey was a 'reactionary old bore'. They corresponded, arguing violently. Shelley also wrote a skit on Wordsworth's poem 'Peter Bell', attacking him together with other high Tories.

'Towards the head of these Dales', wrote Wordsworth in his *Guide*, 'was found a perfect Republic of Shepherds and Agriculturists, among whom the plough of each man was confined to the maintenance of his own family, or to the occasional accommodation of his neighbour. Two or three cows furnished each family with milk and cheese. The chapel was the only edifice that presided over these dwellings, the supreme head of this pure Commonwealth; the members of which existed in the midst of a powerful empire like an ideal society or an organized community, whose constitution had been imposed and regulated by the mountains which protected it.'

The 'perfect Republic' had changed somewhat when the three photographs here were taken. All are by Henry Mayson, the Keswick photographer, who could trace his family back in the Keswick area for many generations and who, like many tourism entrepreneurs, realised there was a better living to be had in catering for the visitors rather than keeping a cow and a few sheep. Henry Mayson had his own studio shop in Lake Road, Keswick (next to the famous Abraham brothers), and had a large-scale relief map of the Lake District which drew large crowds (there were three such models in the town). He also ran (surely Wordsworth would have appreciated this) a lending library – a useful place, as many holidaymakers were confined to their boarding houses and hotels for days on end if the Keswick weather was anything near normal.

Greta Hall at Keswick is a building well known to the Wordsworths, for it was here that S.T. Coleridge lived for three years up to 1803, and Robert Southey lived from 1803 until his death in 1843. William and Dorothy visited very often. This was an important centre for the Lake Poets and thus it appears on many postcards. Alfred Pettitt of Keswick took this picture.

Herbert Bell of Ambleside photographed Robert Southey's grave in Crosthwaite churchyard; it had become a place for tourists to visit. Bell's friend Canon Rawnsley was the vicar of Crosthwaite.

'To the River Greta, near Keswick'

Greta, what fearful listening! when huge stones
Rumble along thy bed, block after block:
Or, whirling with reiterated shock,
Combat, while darkness aggravates the groans:
But if thou (like Cocytus from the moans
Heard on his rueful margin) thence wert named
The Mourner, thy true nature was defamed,
And the habitual murmur that atones
For thy worst rage, forgotten. Oft as Spring
Decks, on thy sinuous banks, her thousand thrones,
Seats of glad instinct and love's carolling,
The concert, for the happy, then may vie
With liveliest peals of birth-day harmony:
To a grieved heart, the notes are benisons.

Herbert Bell of Ambleside photographed the hamlet of Seatoller in the late nineteenth century. At Seatoller House, from around 1860, the Pepper family entertained literary academics, including Wordsworth university scholars (the Wordsworthians).

Opposite: Mary Wilson, Maggie Wildridge and Netta sit very close to the waters of Lodore falls in 1909. Wordsworth had written:

> Far from my dearest friend, 'tis mine to rove
> Through bare grey dell, high wood, and pastoral cove;
> Where Derwent rests and listens to the roar
> That stuns the tremulous cliffs of high Lodore . . .

Another photograph by Herbert Bell shows Watendlath farm buildings. The place gets scant mention in William's *Guide*. He says: 'There are fine bird's eye views from the Castle-hill; from Ashness on the road to Watenlath, and by following the Watenlath stream downwards. . . .'

In her *Journal* for Friday 8 August 1800 Dorothy writes: 'Drank tea at Mr Simpson's, and walked over the mountains at Wattendlath. Very fine gooseberries at Mr S's. A most enchanting walk. Wattendlath, a heavenly scene.'

In Borrowdale, near Keswick, William is reported to have stayed at the Rosthwaite Inn, where he shared a bed with 'a Scotch pedlar'.

Skiddaw, where the poet leaves Benjamin on the road to Keswick, whilst his muse, in 'The Waggoner':

> Beholds the faeries in array,
> Whose party-coloured garments gay
> The silent company betray:
> Red, green, and blue; a moment's sight!
> For Skiddaw-top with rosy light
> Is touched – and all the band take flight.

Herbert Bell pictured the area of Scafell and sold both postcards and lantern slides of the views. Above is Styhead and Great End and to the left Scafell. Wordsworth includes 'excursions' in his *Guide* and one is the description of an ascent of Scafell Pike with a shepherd guide from Rosthwaite in Borrowdale. Wordsworth's friend Coleridge described how he nearly came to a sticky end trying to get from Scafell to Scafell Pike. The poet would have been pleased that his grandson Gordon was involved in the purchase of the summit of Scafell Pike, and its presentation to the National Trust.

Verbosity reigns where Wordsworth's *Guide* includes 'Miscellaneous Observations' of the Lakes:

'As to the order in which objects are best seen – a lake being composed of water flowing from higher grounds, and expanding itself till its receptacle is filled to the brim, – it follows that it will appear to most advantage when approached from its outlet, especially if the lake be in a mountainous country; for, by this way of approach the traveller faces the grander feature of the scene, and is gradually conducted into its most sublime recesses. Now, everyone knows that from amenity and beauty the transition to sublimity is easy and favourable; but the reverse is not so; for, after the faculties have been elevated they are indisposed to humbler excitement.

'The only instances to which the foregoing instances do not apply are Derwent-water and Lowes-water. Derwent is distinguished from all the other Lakes by being surrounded with sublimity: the fantastic mountains of Borrowdale to the south, the solitary of Skiddaw to the north, the bold steeps of Wallow-crag and Lodore to the east, and to the west the clustering mountains of New-lands. . . . Yet as far as respects the formation of such receptacles, the general observation holds good: neither Derwent nor Lowes-water derive any supplies from the streams of those mountains that dignify the landscape towards the outlets.'

The picture shows Derwentwater.

Alfred Pettitt of Keswick caught these children on the Stair Bridge at Newlands, Keswick, and Henry Mayson of Keswick pictured the tourist charabancs (below) climbing Honister from Seatoller. In his *Guide* the poet talks of the poor roads and also the bridges: 'Travellers, who may not have been accustomed to pay attention to things so inobtrusive, will excuse me if I point out the proportions between the span and elevation of the arch, the lightness of the parapet, and the graceful manner in which its curve follows faithfully that of the arch.'

Lowther Castle (above) and Brougham Hall (below) had adjoining estates and are now both in ruins. Lowther Castle was the home of the Lowther family, who employed both William's grandfather and father. Initially William fought 'Wicked Jimmy' Lowther to regain, for the family, money owed to his father. The Brougham family were notable Whigs, and when William came under the influence of the Lowthers in his later life, becoming a Tory and agent of the Lowthers, buying property to create votes, Lord Brougham watched his activities with interest. His magazine *The Edinburgh Review* was very critical of both William's poetry and his private life. The Whig Reform Acts had William completely confused, and he adopted a position absolutely opposite to the one he would have held as a young man.

Abrahams of Keswick sold this picture of Thomas De Quincey as one of their large range of picture postcards. De Quincey was a fan of Wordsworth's poetry from a young age, had a similar disturbed youth and ended up almost part of the Wordsworth family. His addiction to drugs was, like that of Coleridge, a problem for the Wordsworths. He became the editor of the Tory pre-Reform Act paper the *Westmorland Gazette*, which Lowther founded in Kendal as none of the other papers would support him. He wrote a book, *Recollections of the Lake Poets*, in which he gave rather frank views on William. He lived in Dove Cottage for nearly thirty years, moving in when the Wordsworths left for a bigger home.

THE DUDDON

Of all the Lakes area, the valley of the Duddon appears to have raised 'the muse' in Wordsworth like no other place. From 1818 to 1820 he put together his 'Duddon sonnets', which received much applause.

Pure flow the verse, pure, vigorous, free, and bright,
For Duddon, long loved Duddon is my theme. . . .

Artists and photographers followed in
William's footsteps and fame. Many used titles
for their pictures such as 'Wordsworth's
Stepping Stones, Duddon', which are depicted
here.

'The Stepping Stones'

The struggling Rill insensibly is grown
Into a Brook of loud and stately march,
Crossed ever and anon by plank or arch;
And, for like use, lo! what might seem a zone
Chosen for ornament – stone matched with stone
In studied symmetry, with interspace
For the clear waters to pursue their race
Without restraint. How swiftly have they flown,
Succeeding – still succeeding! Here the Child
Puts, when the high-swoln Flood runs fierce and wild,
His budding courage to the proof; and here
Declining Manhood learns to note the sly
And sure encroachments of infirmity,
Thinking how fast time runs, life's end how near!

Guidebooks of the late nineteenth century also drew their readers to the Duddon, with entries such as:

'The Duddon valley has special interest for devout Wordsworthians as the scene of the "Duddon Sonnets" in which the poet traces it down, in thirty-four sonnets, from its source to the sea. The sonnets, it is true, are not, as a rule, particularly happy, though fine lines occur here and there, but the last one of all – entitled "An After Thought" – rises to the very high watermark of great poetry – higher, says Mr Matthew Arnold, than ever rose even Milton. The poet tells us, in an interesting preface, how he first became acquainted with the river, having gone fishing there with a person living in the neighbourhood of Hawkshead when a lad at the Grammar School there. "We fished a great part of the day with very sorry success, the rain pouring torrents, and long before we got home I was worn out with fatigue; and if the good man had not carried me on his back, I must have lain down under the best shelter I could."'

Pearson's Guide goes on to explain how Mrs Wordsworth was lost on another trip and the poet suffered vexation and distress, 'especially to me which I should be ashamed to have recorded for I lost my temper entirely'.

Pearson's Guide continues:

'There is a road, of sorts, for the whole distance of 23¼ miles from Ambleside to Broughton and it is just possible to go over it with a bicycle – we confess to having done it ourselves – between Seathwaite and Broughton the surface is fair but hilly. Portions of course are exceedingly dangerous to careless and inexpert riders, and there are gates across the road in unexpected and awkward positions. – A good walker may easily leave Ambleside early in the morning and be in time to catch the afternoon train and boat back from Broughton. The Broughton road continues down the valley keeping the river on the right, we call it "road" by courtesy; but in sober truth it is nothing better than a cart track leading over the meadows, from gate to gate and from farm to farm.'

The bridges on this route also appeared in these picture postcards of those days.

O Mountain Stream! the Shepherd and his Cot
Are privileged Inmates of deep solitude;
Nor would the nicest Anchorite exclude
A field or two of brighter green, or plot
Of tillage-ground, that seemeth like a spot
Of stationary sunshine: – thou hast viewed
These only, Duddon! with their paths renewed
By fits and starts, yet this contents thee not.
Thee hath some awful Spirit impelled to leave,
Utterly to desert, the haunts of men,
Though simple thy companions were and few;
And through this wilderness a passage cleave
Attended but by thy own voice, save when
The clouds and fowls of the air thy way pursue!

'Tradition'

A love-lorn Maid, at some far-distant time,
Came to this hidden pool, whose depths surpass
In crystal clearness Dian's looking-glass;
And, gazing, saw that rose, which from the prime
Derives its name, reflected as the chime
Of echo doth reverberate some sweet sound:
The starry treasure from the blue profound
She longed to ravish; – shall she plunge, or climb
The humid precipice, and seize the guest
Of April, smiling high in upper air?
Desperate alternative! what fiend could dare
To prompt the thought? – Upon the steep rock's breast
The lonely Primrose yet renews its bloom,
Untouched memento of her hapless doom!

In an unfettered sentence the late Revd F.A. Malleson, vicar of Broughton-in-Furness, wrote in about 1905 in his *Wordsworth and the Duddon* of the river near Birks, where our photograph shows farmers rescuing a crag-fast lamb:

'From sedgy banks varied with the aromatic bog-myrtle, the golden-bog asphodel, now out of flower, the rosy red-rattle, and the milk-white green-veined parnassia, the river comes plunging in haste among wave-washed rocks, and boulders, scooped into fantastic shapes, whitened with weather and the water, then passes on for a few yards through a deep, dark chasm between perpendicular rocks, cleft with gloomy fissures, deeper and deeper, narrower and more narrow, not, at any rate today, without hurry to a black pit some twenty feet deep, spanned aloft by one narrow arch; and here an exclamation of surprise spontaneously bursts forth, even from a solitary wanderer as he gazes down with astonishment into the intense transparency of the emerald green of that pellucid pool, where now the water lags lazily along only indicating the sluggishness of its movement by the gentle wafting of small discs of white foam brought from the fall close by.'

'After-thought'

I thought of thee, my partner and my guide,
As being past away. — Vain sympathies!
For, backward, Duddon! as I cast my eyes,
I see what was, and is, and will abide;
Still glides the Stream, and shall for ever glide;
The Form remains, the Function never dies;
While we, the brave, the mighty, and the wise,
We Men, who in our morn of youth defied
The elements, must vanish; — be it so!
Enough, if something from our hands hath power
To live, and act, and serve the future hour;
And if, as toward the silent tomb we go,
Through love, through hope, and faith's transcendent dower,
We feel that we are greater than we know.

'Seathwaite Chapel'

Sacred Religion! 'mother of form and fear,'
Dread arbitress of mutable respect,
New rites ordaining when the old are wrecked,
Or cease to please the fickle worshipper;
Mother of Love! (that name best suits thee here)
Mother of Love! for this deep vale, protect
Truth's holy lamp, pure source of bright effect,
Gifted to purge the vapoury atmosphere
That seeks to stifle it; – as in those days
When this low Pile a Gospel Teacher knew,
Whose good works formed an endless retinue;
A Pastor such as Chaucer's verse pourtrays;
Such as the heaven-taught skill of Herbert drew;
And tender Goldsmith crowned with deathless praise!

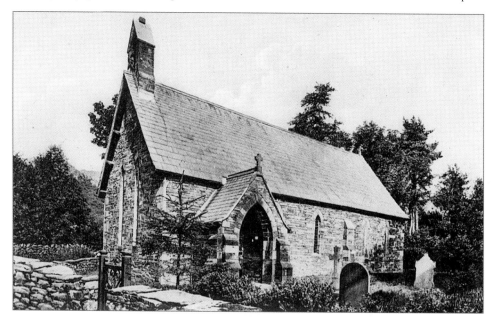

THE *GUIDE*

Drawing by H.W. Pickersgill, 1832.

'Those who wish to see the celebrated ruins of Furness Abbey, and are not afraid of crossing the sands, may go from Lancaster to Ulverston; from which place take the direct road to Dalton; but by all means return through Urswick for the sake of the view from the top of the hill, before descending into the grounds of Conishead Priory.' This is from the 'Directions for the Tourist' at the beginning of Wordsworth's *Guide to the Lakes*. William returns to the crossing of the sands in 'The Prelude':

> Of vehicles and travellers horse and foot,
> Wading beneath the conduct of their guide . . .

Conishead Priory, a mansion built on the site of a medieval priory, features on many of the first picture postcards of the area either as a drawing (as above) or as a photograph. This is a cottage in the grounds.

The ruins of Furness Abbey feature a number of times in the *Guide* and in other works by the poet. In the *Guide* he quotes extensively from Father Thomas West's earlier guides. The following three photographs are from the time before the abbey ruins came into the care of the Ministry of Works; the picture on p. 140 is by Herbert Bell of Ambleside. All depict the overgrown (and romantic?) ruins that William would have known.

'At Furness Abbey'

Here, where, of havoc tired and rash undoing,
Man left this Structure to become Time's prey,
A soothing spirit follows in the way
That Nature takes, her counter-work pursuing.
See how her Ivy clasps the sacred Ruin,
Fall to prevent or beautify decay;
And, on the mouldered walls, how bright, how gay,
The flowers in pearly dews their bloom renewing!
Thanks to the place, blessings upon the hour;
Even as I speak the rising Sun's first smile
Gleams on the grass-crowned top of yon tall Tower,
Whose cawing occupants with joy proclaim
Prescriptive title to the shattered pile,
Where, Cavendish, *thine* seems nothing but a name!

The *Guide* has little to say about the ruins of the Cistercian abbey at Calder. 'This road to Wastdale, after passing the village of Lamplugh Cross, presents suddenly a fine view of the Lake of Ennerdale, with its Mountains; and six, or seven miles beyond, leads down to Calder Abbey. Little of this ruin is left, but that little is well worthy of notice.' One must query William's comment that 'little of this ruin is left'.

The story of the destruction of this Lakeland valley in the cause of water supply has been told many times. Wordsworth's *Guide*'s comment, 'From Pooley Bridge at the foot of the lake [Ullswater], Haweswater may be conveniently visited. Haweswater is a lesser Ullswater, with this advantage, that it remains undefiled by the intrusion of bad taste', makes a poignant record in view of the subsequent events. Photographer Lowe of Patterdale recorded (above) the lake at its natural level and (below) the lost church at Mardale.

The Low Wood Hotel came into the Logan family during the lifetime of the poet, but had been a roadside coaching hotel for some time before that. It was much enlarged in 1859. John Logan married Richard Rigg's daughter and so the famous coaching family also had an interest in the establishment. Herbert Bell of Ambleside took this picture for his lantern slide series. Wordsworth's *Guide* includes the hotel, giving it a special place in the narrative:

'Low-wood Inn, a mile from the head of Windermere, is a most pleasant halting-place; no Inn in the district is so agreeably situated for water views and excursions; and the fields about it, and the lanes that lead to Troutbeck, present beautiful views towards each extremity of the Lake.'

The *Guide* has much to say about Hartsop:

'Lastly having gone along the western side of Brothers-water and passed Hartsop Hall, a stream soon after issues from a cove richly decorated with native wood. This spot is, I believe, never explored by Travellers; but, from these sylvan and rocky recesses, whoever looks back on the gleaming surface of Brothers-water, or forward to the precipitous sides and lofty ridges of Dove Crag, etc, will be equally pleased with the beauty, the grandeur, and the wildness of the scenery. – one of which [streams] would lead up from a point where it crosses the Kirkstone-road, near the foot of Brothers-water, to the decaying hamlet of Hartsop, remarkable for its cottage architecture. . . .'

Lowe of Patterdale photographed this 'spinning gallery'.

The interior of the cottages of the farmers of Lakeland, the cottages which took up a number of pages in Wordsworth's *Guide*, also attracted the attention of the early local postcard photographers. Above is an interior view of Brotherinkeld, Eskdale, pictured by G.P. Abraham of Keswick, and below is Lane Head, Ullswater, by Lowe of Patterdale. It is as well that scenes such as these were recorded, as a combination of a wish to modernise combined with the value of seventeenth- and eighteenth-century locally carved furniture has stripped many such an interior.

612 ._ "Long Meg" near Penrith
(Abraham's Series)

'The daughters of Long Meg are placed not in an oblong, as the stones of Shap, but in a perfect circle eighty yards in diameter and seventy two in number, and from above three yards high, to less than so many feet: a little way out of the circle stands LONG MEG herself – a single stone eighteen feet high. . . .' reads William's *Guide*. He continues: 'When the author first saw this monument, he came upon it by surprise, therefore might overrate its importance as an object; but he must say, that though it is not to be compared with Stonehenge, he has not seen any other remains of those dark ages, which can pretend to rival it in singularity and dignity of appearance.' Then follows a sonnet, starting as follows:

> A weight of awe, not easy to be borne
> Fell suddenly upon my spirit, cast
> From the dread bosom of the unknown past,
> When I first saw that sisterhood forlorn. . . .

Opposite: 'Into Wastdale are three roads,' says the *Guide*, 'viz. over the Stye from Borrowdale; a short cut from Eskdale by Burnmoor Tarn, which road descends on the head of the Lake; and the principal entrance from the open country by the Strands at its foot. The last is much the best approach. Wastdale is well worth the notice of the Traveller who is not afraid of fatigue; no part of the country is more distinguished by sublimity.'

Herbert Bell of Ambleside caught that sublimity in his photograph.

'This lake also, if the weather be fine, ought to be circumnavigated' reads the *Guide*. 'There are good views along the western side of Bassenthwaite Lake, and from Armathwaite at its foot; but the eastern side from the high road has little to recommend it. The Traveller from Carlisle, approaching from the way of Ireby, has, from the old road on the top of Bassenthwaite-hawse, much the most striking view of the Plain and Lake of Bassenthwaite, flanked by Skiddaw, and terminated by Wallow Crag on the south east of Derwent Lake.'

Henry Mayson of Keswick's delightful view is from the recommended western side.

'The Mountains of the Vale of Buttermere and Crummock are nowhere so impressive as from the bosom of Crummock water,' reads the *Guide*, and passes on to other things. At least Wordsworth returns to the area in his 'Prelude' and talks about the Maid of Buttermere:

> And how, unfaithful to a virtuous wife,
> Deserted and deceived, the Spoiler came
> And wooed the artless daughter of the hills. . . .

In the centre of this photograph of late nineteenth-century Langdale is a plantation of fir trees, cleared at the time of the First World War. Wordsworth's *Guide* has much advice to give on the planting of trees in the Lake District. 'Larch and fir plantations have been spread, not merely with a view to profit, but in many instances for the sake of ornament. To those who plant for profit, and are thrusting every other tree out of the way, to make room for their favourite, the larch, I would utter first a regret that they should have selected these lovely vales for their vegetable manufactory, when there is so much barren and irreclaimable land in the neighbouring moors, and in other parts of the Island, which might have been had for this purpose at a far cheaper rate. . . .' A number of pages follow with similar advice.

Opposite: Alfred Pettitt, who started his career in Grasmere before setting up a studio at Keswick, took this remarkable photograph of the coaches on the regular holiday 'round' through Borrowdale and over Honister Pass. Wordsworth's *Guide* does not suggest this route as the best to gain access to Buttermere: 'Buttermere may be visited by a shorter way through Newlands (from Keswick), but though the descent upon the Vale of Buttermere is very striking, as is the one entering by the head of the Vale, under Honister Crag, yet, after all, the best entrance from Keswick is from the lower part of the Vale . . . over Whinlater to Scale Hill where there is a roomy Inn. . . .'

We include the end of the Conclusion to Wordsworth's *Guide to the Lakes*. Readers are invited to indulge themselves in their knowledge of what actually happened after the poet's death in 1850. We are sure that the poet's 'every man's right and interest' did not include the water and mineral extraction, the mass tourism industry, or the new use for the land at Sella Park (or Field), which used to belong to the monks of Calder Abbey nearby.

'The author has been induced to speak thus at length, by a wish to preserve the native beauty of this delightful district, because still further changes in its appearance must inevitably follow, from the change of inhabitants and owners which is rapidly taking place. – About the same time that strangers began to be attracted to the country, and feel a desire to settle in it, the difficulty, that would have stood in their way of their procuring situations, was lessened by an unfortunate alteration in the circumstances of the native peasantry, proceeding from a cause which then began to operate, and is now felt in every house. The family of each man, whether *estatesman* or farmer, formerly had a two fold support; first, the produce of his lands and flocks; and, secondly, the profit drawn from the employment of the women and children, as manufacturers; spinning their own wool in their own houses (work done chiefly in the winter season), and carrying it to market for sale. Hence, however numerous the children, the income of the family kept pace with its increase. But, by the invention and universal application of machinery, this second resource has been cut off; the gains being so far reduced as not to be sought after but by a few aged persons disabled from other employment. Doubtless, the invention of machinery has not been to these people a pure loss; for the profits arising from home manufactures operated as a strong temptation to choose that mode of labour in neglect of husbandry. They also participate in the general benefit which the island has derived from the increased value of the produce of land, brought about by the establishment of manufactories, and in the consequent quickening of the agricultural industry. But this is far from making them amends; and now that home manufactures are nearly done away, though the women and children might, at many seasons of the year, employ themselves with advantage in the fields beyond what they are accustomed to do, yet still all possible exertion in this way cannot be rationally expected from persons whose agricultural knowledge is so confined, and above all, where there must necessarily be so small a capital. The consequence then is – that the proprietors and farmers being no longer able to maintain themselves upon small farms, several are united in one, and the buildings go to decay or are destroyed; and that the lands of the *estatesman* being mortgaged, and the owner constrained to part with them, they fall into hands of wealthy purchasers, who in like manner unite and consolidate; and, if they wish to become residents, erect new mansions out of the ruins of the ancient cottages, whose little enclosures, with all the wild graces that grow out of them, disappear. The feudal tenure under which the estates are held has indeed done something towards checking this influx of new settlers; but so strong is the inclination, that these galling restraints are endured; and it is probable, that in a few years the country at the margin of the Lakes will fall almost entirely into the possession of gentry, either strangers or natives. It is then much to be wished, that a better taste should prevail among these new proprietors; and, as they cannot be expected to leave things to themselves, that skill and knowledge should prevent unnecessary deviations from that path of simplicity and beauty along which, without design and unconsciously, their humble predecessors have moved. In this wish the author will be joined by persons of pure taste throughout the whole island, who, by their visits (often repeated) to the Lakes in the North of England, testify that they deem the district a sort of national property, in which every man has a right and interest who has an eye to perceive and a heart to enjoy.'

POSTSCRIPT

The bust of Wordsworth was also added to the miniature pottery made by firms such as Goss.

Shut close the door; press down the latch,
Sleep in thy intellectual crust;
Nor lose ten tickings of thy watch
Near this unprofitable dust.
                    '*A Poet's Epitaph*'

Mary Hutchinson was a playmate of three-year-old William when they met at Ann Birkett's dame school in Penrith. Her relationship with the Wordsworths is traced in Hunter Davies's biography. She was a great friend of both William and Dorothy, and Dorothy was in correspondence with her for many years until she joined the family by marrying William on 4 October 1802. She survived William to die at eighty-eight years of age in 1859. She had known the poet for most of his life, bore his children and shared the heartbreaks and joys of their married life. After his death she ensured that unpublished material of 'The Prelude' (as she called it) was published. Abrahams of Keswick included her portrait in their postcard series.

It is interesting to compare this picture of the interior of Grasmere church with the one on p. 59. This picture from the early 1930s shows a much neater interior and the Wordsworth memorial (see p. 61) has appeared on the centre wall. In time Rydal church replaced Grasmere as the Wordsworth family's place of worship (see pp. 36–7); he never saw the church at Ambleside, which now has the Wordsworth chapel.

This 1950s picture of the interior of the Wordsworth chapel at St Mary's, Ambleside, shows the two smaller side windows almost completely. These carry dedications to Mary, his wife, Dorothy, his sister, Dora, his daughter, and Sarah Hutchinson, his sister-in-law. The main east window is dedicated to the poet. All inscriptions are in Latin and all windows include at their top the Wordsworth motto 'Veritas' (truth). To the Wordsworth pilgrim seeking his memory in this fine Victorian church it proves to be no satisfactory mecca and the walls of the chapel carry memorials to others. The hundred years' delay in completion seems to show that much of the 1850s enthusiasm quickly waned.

Opposite: Work on a new church in Ambleside, that of St Mary the Virgin, was commenced in the year of William's death and completed in 1854. Sir George Gilbert Scott was the architect, and his original ideas included a Wordsworth memorial chapel. The memorial windows were installed, the main one paid for in 1853–5 by friends and admirers of the poet from Britain and the USA. The chapel itself, though, did not materialise for a hundred years, when it was fitted out at the time of the 1952–4 centenary celebrations of the church. The present seating was completed in 1970.

ACKNOWLEDGEMENTS

We wish to acknowledge the invaluable assistance of the following Lakeland people: the Trustees of the Armitt Library and in particular their volunteer assistant Bernard Wood, expert on the Bell photographic collection; Hunter Davies, who allowed us to use his Wordsworth biography; George Dawson of Kendal, generous as always in the use of his knowledge and large photographic collection; the Kendal Library Local Studies Collection and Jackie Fay, Librarian; and the Wordsworth Trust at Dove Cottage, Grasmere, in particular Mrs Pamela Woof, who allowed us to quote from her book, *The Grasmere Journals Dorothy Wordsworth*, and Jeff Cowton.

We also wish to thank our wives Jean and Barbara, stoical in our enthusiasms.

BRITAIN IN OLD PHOTOGRAPHS

Lincoln
Lincoln Cathedral
The Lincolnshire Coast
Liverpool
Around Llandudno
Around Lochaber
Theatrical London
Around Louth
The Lower Fal Estuary
Lowestoft
Luton
Lympne Airfield
Lytham St Annes
Maidenhead
Around Maidenhead
Around Malvern
Manchester
Manchester Road & Rail
Mansfield
Marlborough: A Second Selection
Marylebone & Paddington
Around Matlock
Melton Mowbray
Around Melksham
The Mendips
Merton & Morden
Middlesbrough
Midsomer Norton & Radstock
Around Mildenhall
Milton Keynes
Minehead
Monmouth & the River Wye
The Nadder Valley
Newark
Around Newark
Newbury
Newport, Isle of Wight
The Norfolk Broads
Norfolk at War
North Fylde
North Lambeth
North Walsham & District
Northallerton
Northampton
Around Norwich
Nottingham 1944–74
The Changing Face of Nottingham
Victorian Nottingham
Nottingham Yesterday & Today
Nuneaton
Around Oakham
Ormskirk & District
Otley & District
Oxford: The University
Oxford Yesterday & Today
Oxfordshire Railways: A Second
   Selection
Oxfordshire at School
Around Padstow
Pattingham & Wombourne

Penwith
Penzance & Newlyn
Around Pershore
Around Plymouth
Poole
Portsmouth
Poulton-le-Fylde
Preston
Prestwich
Pudsey
Radcliffe
RAF Chivenor
RAF Cosford
RAF Hawkinge
RAF Manston
RAF Manston: A Second Selection
RAF St Mawgan
RAF Tangmere
Ramsgate & Thanet Life
Reading
Reading: A Second Selection
Redditch & the Needle District
Redditch: A Second Selection
Richmond, Surrey
Rickmansworth
Around Ripley
The River Soar
Romney Marsh
Romney Marsh: A Second
   Selection
Rossendale
Around Rotherham
Rugby
Around Rugeley
Ruislip
Around Ryde
St Albans
St Andrews
Salford
Salisbury
Salisbury: A Second Selection
Salisbury: A Third Selection
Around Salisbury
Sandhurst & Crowthorne
Sandown & Shanklin
Sandwich
Scarborough
Scunthorpe
Seaton, Lyme Regis & Axminster
Around Seaton & Sidmouth
Sedgley & District
The Severn Vale
Sherwood Forest
Shrewsbury
Shrewsbury: A Second Selection
Shropshire Railways
Skegness
Around Skegness
Skipton & the Dales
Around Slough

Smethwick
Somerton & Langport
Southampton
Southend-on-Sea
Southport
Southwark
Southwell
Southwold to Aldeburgh
Stafford
Around Stafford
Staffordshire Railways
Around Staveley
Stepney
Stevenage
The History of Stilton Cheese
Stoke-on-Trent
Stoke Newington
Stonehouse to Painswick
Around Stony Stratford
Around Stony Stratford: A Second
   Selection
Stowmarket
Streatham
Stroud & the Five Valleys
Stroud & the Five Valleys: A
   Second Selection
Stroud's Golden Valley
The Stroudwater and Thames &
   Severn Canals
The Stroudwater and Thames &
   Severn Canals: A Second
   Selection
Suffolk at Work
Suffolk at Work: A Second
   Selection
The Heart of Suffolk
Sunderland
Sutton
Swansea
Swindon: A Third Selection
Swindon: A Fifth Selection
Around Tamworth
Taunton
Around Taunton
Teesdale
Teesdale: A Second Selection
Tenbury Wells
Around Tettenhall & Codshall
Tewkesbury & the Vale of
   Gloucester
Thame to Watlington
Around Thatcham
Around Thirsk
Thornbury to Berkeley
Tipton
Around Tonbridge
Trowbridge
Around Truro
TT Races
Tunbridge Wells

Tunbridge Wells: A Second
   Selection
Twickenham
Uley, Dursley & Cam
The Upper Fal
The Upper Tywi Valley
Uxbridge, Hillingdon & Cowley
The Vale of Belvoir
The Vale of Conway
Ventnor
Wakefield
Wallingford
Walsall
Waltham Abbey
Wandsworth at War
Wantage, Faringdon & the Vale
   Villages
Around Warwick
Weardale
Weardale: A Second Selection
Wednesbury
Wells
Welshpool
West Bromwich
West Wight
Weston-super-Mare
Around Weston-super-Mare
Weymouth & Portland
Around Wheatley
Around Whetstone
Whitchurch to Market Drayton
Around Whitstable
Wigton & the Solway Plain
Willesden
Around Wilton
Wimbledon
Around Windsor
Wingham, Addisham &
   Littlebourne
Wisbech
Witham & District
Witney
Around Witney
The Witney District
Wokingham
Around Woodbridge
Around Woodstock
Woolwich
Woolwich Royal Arsenal
Around Wootton Bassett,
   Cricklade & Purton
Worcester
Worcester in a Day
Around Worcester
Worcestershire at Work
Around Worthing
Wotton-under-Edge to Chipping
   Sodbury
Wymondham & Attleborough
The Yorkshire Wolds

To order any of these titles please telephone our distributor, Littlehampton Book Services on 01903 721596
For a catalogue of these and our other titles please ring Regina Schinner on 01453 731114